Sir Francis Drake

and the Foundation of a World Empire

Explorers of New Worlds

Sir Francis Drake

and the Foundation
of a World Empire

Jim Gallagher

Chelsea House Publishers
Philadelphia

To Anne, my favorite sister.

Prepared for Chelsea House Publishers by:
OTTN Publishing, Stockton, N.J.

CHELSEA HOUSE PUBLISHERS
Production Manager: Pamela Loos
Art Director: Sara Davis
Director of Photography: Judy L. Hasday
Managing Editor: James D. Gallagher
Senior Production Editor: J. Christopher Higgins
Series Designer: Keith Trego
Cover Design: Forman Group

3 5 7 9 8 6 4 2

Library of Congress Cataloging-in-Publication Data

Gallagher, Jim, 1969-
    Sir Francis Drake and the foundation of a world
    empire / Jim Gallagher
        p.   cm. – (Explorers of new worlds)
Includes bibliographical references and index.
ISBN 0-7910-5950-2 (hc) – ISBN 0-7910-6160-4 (pb)
1. Drake, Sir Francis, 1540?-1596–Juvenile literature.
2. Explorers–America–Biography–Juvenile literature.
3. America–Discovery and exploration–British–Juvenile
literature. 4. Explorers–Great Britain–Biography–Juvenile literature. 5. Admirals–Great Britain–Biography–
Juvenile literature. [1. Drake, Sir Francis, 1540?-1596.
2. Explorers. 3. Admirals.] I. Title. II. Series.

E129.D7.G35 2000
942.05'5'092–dc21
[B]   00-043073

Contents

Master Thief of the Unknown World I

The fishermen on a small boat bobbing in the waters off Plymouth, a port city in England, were surprised to see a well-weathered ship sailing toward them. The September afternoon sun was sinking into the west as the two-masted vessel pulled alongside. A broad-shouldered, bearded man peered down at them from the deck. He had curly, reddish hair, and a scar from an arrow wound on his right cheek. "Is the Queen still alive?" he shouted to the fishermen.

When the English fishermen answered "yes," the powerfully built captain relaxed. His name was Francis Drake.

When his ship, the *Golden Hind,* landed at Plymouth harbor on September 26, 1580, Drake became the first Englishman to lead a sailing expedition completely around the world. He had started from Plymouth nearly three years earlier with five ships, but only one had completed the journey.

The hold of Drake's ship was loaded with valuable cargo: gold and silver, **spices**, jewels, fine porcelain, and rare maps. Drake had collected these riches by raiding Spanish ships and towns in the New World. He was not ready to unload his cargo yet, however. First he had to see what the political situation was in his home country.

When Drake had set out, there was an uneasy peace between England and Spain. The queen of England, Elizabeth I, had secretly approved Drake's plan to harass Spain's New World outposts. However, Drake knew the Spanish were very angry about his attacks. If Spain and England were on friendly terms, Queen

The first man to lead a voyage around the world was Ferdinand Magellan. However, Magellan had died before the journey was finished in 1522. During the next 58 years, no one else was able to complete the dangerous voyage until Francis Drake.

Elizabeth would have to pretend she had not known about, or approved, Drake's voyage. The brave sailor's reward might come at the hands of the executioner!

Cautiously, he sent for his wife and the mayor of Plymouth. He learned that both friends and enemies had been waiting to hear of his arrival. Drake decided to send a secret message to the queen in London. He would hide out until he learned what she was thinking.

Drake did not tell his crew that he might be in trouble. Instead, he reported that there was an outbreak of the plague in Plymouth (this, in fact, was true). The *Golden Hind* sailed to a small, deserted island in the English Channel. Today, the island where Francis Drake and his men waited for word from London is known as Drake's Island.

The political situation was uncertain. Spain was the most powerful country in the world at the time. The discoveries of Christopher Columbus, Ferdinand Magellan, and others had given Spain control of a vast empire in the New World and made it the richest nation in Europe. By contrast, England was a small, weak country. It was not prepared for a war with Spain.

When Queen Elizabeth received Drake's message, she was curious. The clever sailor had listed all of the valuable items he had brought. Drake also reported that he had made great geographical discoveries that he would share with Elizabeth. She invited Drake to come to the royal court, telling him he had nothing to fear.

During a six-hour interview, Drake showed the queen his diary, which was filled with drawings and paintings of new lands, people, and animals discovered in her name. Drake had found another route from the Atlantic to the Pacific Ocean. He had also sailed along the west coast of North America and proved that there was no "northwest passage," as most geographers of the time believed. Drake had claimed a large area of land on the Pacific coast of North America in the queen's name, calling it "New Albion." And he negotiated trading treaties with several nations in the East Indies before returning home.

The queen was under pressure from Spain to return the treasure Drake had taken. However, she defied the country's powerful ruler, King Philip II. She refused to return the treasure, and she also started talking with the rulers of France about an *alliance*. France and Spain were enemies, so this was practically a declaration of war. But the biggest insult was yet to come.

On April 1, 1581, the *Golden Hind* sailed up the Thames River toward London. Its tattered sails had been replaced with brightly colored banners. Silk streamers with the royal crest flew from the ship. Even the crew was well-scrubbed. The *Golden Hind* had been prepared for a visit by Queen Elizabeth.

As Drake knelt before his queen, she held a golden sword over his neck. "My royal brother, the King of Spain, has demanded your head," she announced. The crowd gasped. Then Elizabeth handed the sword to a French nobleman, Monsieur de Marchaumont, who stood at her side. Smiling, the queen said, "We shall ask Monsieur to be the headsman."

Marchaumont tapped the blade on Drake's shoulders and pronounced the sailor a knight of England, saying, "Arise, Sir Knight, the master thief of the unknown world."

This portrait of Sir Francis Drake was painted while he was still alive. Drake was born to a poor family, but his sailing skill and daring bravery would make him one of the most famous Englishmen of his age.

Spain and the Sea

2

rancis Drake was born in a small cabin near the English town of Tavistock, 20 miles from the busy port of Plymouth. The exact year of his birth is unknown. Many historians believe it was 1541, although he may have been born as early as 1538 or as late as 1546. In 1549 the Drakes moved to Chatham, a town near London that was the site of England's main shipyard.

Francis Drake never attended school. He was taught to read and write by his father, Edmund. The rest of his education came from listening to the sailors who regularly visited Chatham. He heard about new lands that had been discovered to the east and west. He learned about the sea and about sailors' superstitions. And he learned about life in other countries, such as Spain, which had built a powerful empire.

After Christopher Columbus discovered the Americas in 1492, Spain had sent soldiers to explore this "New World" and exploit its resources. *Conquistadors* such as Hernando Cortés and Francisco Pizarro successfully enslaved native populations and forced them to mine gold and silver. The Spanish king, Charles V, used these riches to build a powerful empire. By the time his son, Philip, came to the throne, Spain controlled most of Europe.

England, by contrast, was a weak country torn by religious wars. The country was not stabilized until 1558, when Queen Elizabeth I came to power. The new English queen was smart and ambitious. She began working to make her country strong enough to rival Spain.

In the meantime, however, Francis Drake began to learn about the sea. His father made a deal with the owner of a small cargo boat. The captain would take 12-year-old Francis on as his *apprentice*. Francis would have to work on the ship full-time. In exchange, the captain would teach him about the sea and provide food and a place for him to live.

For many, life as an apprentice was downright unpleasant. Francis, however, was luckier than most. His master was a kind, older man who did not have a wife or children. He took a liking to his young apprentice.

There was a lot for Francis to learn. The captain

Two of the most powerful European rulers of the 16th century: King Philip II of Spain and Queen Elizabeth of England.

taught him about currents and tides, how to read a compass, and how to navigate using the sun and stars. Francis also learned how to handle the small ship in all kinds of weather. The ship Francis Drake was apprenticed to was used to haul coal and timber across the English Channel to France and the Netherlands.

In 1560, Francis Drake's master died. In his will, the old captain left his ship to his apprentice. Drake spent the next few years as master of the ship. Although he made a good living steering his trading ship across the English Channel, Drake became bored. He sold his ship and moved to Plymouth.

Drake hoped to find adventure with the help of a family to whom he was distantly related. The Hawkins family owned many trading ships. William Hawkins had been a naval advisor to King Henry VIII. His son John had earned his own reputation on two voyages between 1562 and 1565. He had sailed to Africa and picked up slaves, then traveled to the New World and sold the slaves to Spanish colonists in the Caribbean. These slave-trading trips, the first by an Englishman, were very profitable.

In 1566, Francis Drake made his first voyage to the New World. He was second in command of a

Sir John Hawkins was a member of an influential seagoing family. His father, William, had made the first English voyages to Brazil. John Hawkins was in charge of his family's fleet of ships. He made his reputation with profitable slave-trading voyages in 1562 and 1565.

ship owned by the Hawkins family. Under the captain, John Lovell, Drake learned about **navigation** on the open sea. He also took part in his first sea fighting. His ship attacked Portuguese vessels and seized the valuable cargoes they were carrying— slaves, ivory, wax, and sugar.

However, when Lovell's ship reached the Spanish Main, as the waters around the Caribbean islands and the coasts of South and Central America were known, its crew was in for disappointment. In the past, Hawkins's well-armed fleets of ships had forced Spanish towns to trade for the slaves he had kidnapped from Portuguese ships. This time the English were not strong enough to threaten force. Lovell was forced to return home empty-handed.

When they arrived in Plymouth in September 1567, Hawkins was preparing another voyage to the Caribbean. This time, his six-ship fleet would include warships. The two largest ships were the 26-gun *Jesus of Lubeck* and the 24-gun *Minion.* John Hawkins himself would command the expedition from the *Jesus of Lubeck.* Drake was hired as one of the officers on Hawkins's **flagship**.

The Englishmen raided Portuguese settlements in the Cape Verde Islands and along the coast of Africa. They captured men who could be sold as slaves in the New World. The English also increased the size of their fleet by capturing three Portuguese ships. Drake was placed in command of one of these, the *Gratia Dei* (Grace of God). He would later become captain of a larger ship, the *Judith.* When a French pirate joined the English fleet, its number was increased to 10 ships.

By the time Hawkins's fleet sailed west for the Caribbean, about 400 slaves were chained below the ships' decks. In March 1568, the English reached the New World.

The first stop to sell slaves was the port of Borburata. However, the Spanish living in the New World had been ordered not to buy slaves from English traders. The colonial governor of Borburata turned down Hawkins's trade offer.

Next stop was Rio de la Hacha. Hawkins sent two ships, the *Judith* and the *Angel,* ahead to the port. The Spanish fired at the English ships. Drake responded by ordering the *Judith*'s gunners to shoot a cannonball through the house of the town's governor, Miguel de Castellanos.

The rest of the fleet arrived a few days later. Hawkins asked Castellanos for permission to sell his slaves, but the Spaniard refused. Hawkins ordered an attack the next day, and 200 well-armed Englishmen captured Rio de la Hacha. Hawkins forced the Spanish to buy about 200 slaves. Castellanos also had to pay Hawkins a ransom to keep the English sailors from destroying the town.

There was no resistance at the next Spanish town, Santa Marta. The colonists there desperately needed slaves, so they ignored the Spanish laws against trade with English slavers. Hawkins and his men sold about 110 slaves in Santa Marta before departing.

The English ships stopped at other towns on the Spanish Main, but they could not sell all of the slaves. Eventually, Hawkins decided to sail for home. Even though the English still held nearly 60 slaves captive, they had collected enough gold, silver, and pearls to show a profit for the voyage. Hawkins sank one of the captured Portuguese ships, and the French pirates left the fleet with their share of the booty. Down to eight ships, the fleet set a course for England.

A violent storm ruined Hawkins's plan. The ships were blown far off course, into the Gulf of Mexico. One of the ships, the *William and John,* was separated from the others and eventually returned to England. Several of the remaining seven English ships were damaged, including the *Jesus of Lubeck,* which was leaking badly. Hawkins had no choice but to find a port where repairs could be made. Otherwise, the ships would never survive the return voyage across the Atlantic.

The closest port was San Juan de Ulúa. This was a small but important town, because the Spanish *flota* stopped there. The *flota* was a group of many vessels carrying treasure from the New World to Spain. It was guarded by powerful warships.

The guarded gate to the Spanish city of San Juan de Ulúa, located on the Gulf Coast of Mexico. Hawkins and Drake were forced to sail to the Spanish port in order to repair their storm-damaged ships.

Hawkins hoped the repairs could be finished before the *flota* arrived.

Four days after the seven English ships arrived in San Juan de Ulúa, the masts of numerous ships could be seen out at sea—the *flota* was approaching. Hawkins drew cannons into position and prepared his men for battle, but he did not want to attack the *flota.* That might provoke a war between England and Spain and would surely anger the queen. Instead, he wanted to control access to the harbor. He could refuse to let the Spanish enter until they agreed to let him complete his repairs and leave San Juan de Ulúa in peace.

When the *flota* arrived, it was carrying the new viceroy, or ruler, of Mexico, Don Martin Enriquez. The viceroy was angry when he learned that the English controlled San Juan de Ulúa. However, Enriquez had to agree to Hawkins's demands. Soon the Spanish ships were crowded into the harbor next to the English vessels.

Enriquez did not intend to let the English leave without a fight, though. These were Spanish waters, and it was his duty to rid them of enemies like Hawkins and Drake. The Spaniards secretly planned a surprise attack.

On September 23, 1568, the attack began. Spanish soldiers swarmed over the deck of the *Minion,* and the other English ships were raked with cannon and musket fire. The English sailors on board the *Minion* fought back fiercely, repelling the attackers.

The English ships took a terrible beating from Spanish cannon fire. The *Jesus of Lubeck* was badly damaged, and the other ships were disabled or sunk. Drake was fortunate: his ship, the *Judith,* was the farthest away from the Spanish cannons and suffered little damage.

On the *Jesus of Lubeck,* Hawkins supervised the transfer of treasure to the *Minion* and the *Judith.* He and his crew then left the battered warship for the other two ships and sailed from the harbor.

In the night, as the ships attempted to get away from the Spanish town, the *Minion* and the *Judith* were separated. Drake, although inexperienced at ocean navigation, decided to put out to sea. It took him four months to cross the Atlantic and return to England with his men. Hawkins also survived, although many of his men did not. Some had asked to be put ashore in the New World rather than take the risky return voyage in the overcrowded *Minion.* Most of the English sailors who were captured by the Spanish in San Juan de Ulúa were enslaved or put to death.

The Treasure House of the World 3

Drake wanted revenge for the humiliating defeat at San Juan de Ulúa. He begged Queen Elizabeth to let him lead a fleet of English warships against the Spanish colonies. However, the queen did not want war with Spain, and she refused.

Drake decided that he would continue to fight against Spain—without the queen's support. He would return to the Caribbean and become a pirate, taking as much of Spain's New World gold and silver as his ship could hold.

In 1570, Drake sailed back to the Caribbean. He did not raid any Spanish ships or settlements on this voyage.

Instead, he gathered information. His first target would be the Spanish town of Nombre de Dios, a small port in Panama. The port was the starting point of the other Spanish *flota* that took gold and silver mined in South America to Spain each year. Drake called it the "treasure house of the world."

After returning to England, Drake outfitted a ship, the *Swan*. In February 1571, he sailed back to the Caribbean. This time, he was ready to fight. On Drake's first raid, he captured a Spanish frigate. The ship's crew was so frightened at Drake's approach that they fled the ship. Drake took all the valuable items he found, then left a note of warning for the Spanish. In it, the English captain said he would be fair to any Spaniard who surrendered when attacked. If they caused his crew to fight, however, "we will be devils rather than men," he wrote.

After this, Drake and his men took several small boats up the Chagres River to the Spanish town of Venta Cruces. They sank several larger Spanish ships and seized their goods. Returning downstream to Nombre de Dios, Drake's men continued to capture valuable cargoes. Between raids, Drake's men anchored their ship in a sheltered bay east of Nombre de Dios. Drake called the camp Port Pheasant.

A replica of a Spanish galleon. Although these large ships could carry a great deal of treasure, they were easy prey for fast, well-armed ships such as Drake's.

The Spanish colonists were terrified at these lightning raids. They set urgent messages to King Philip in Spain, asking for protection. Although Spain sent out three well-armed search parties, they could not find Drake. He sailed back to England in June 1571. His ship was filled with Spanish treasure.

In May 1572, Drake was ready to make his most daring voyage yet. This time, he had 73 men and an additional ship. His new vessel, the *Pasco*, was three times as large as the *Swan* and had 12 cannons.

Drake's 1571 raid was so successful that at least 30 other English captains were inspired to attack Spanish ships and towns in the New World.

Drake commanded the *Pasco*, while his brother John was captain of the *Swan*.

When the ships arrived in the Caribbean, they found that Port Pheasant had been discovered by the Spanish. Drake found a new hiding place and set his men to work building a small fort. They also put together three *pinnaces*–small sailboats that could be broken down and carried in a larger ship, then assembled quickly when needed. While they were working, an English captain named James Raunse arrived at Drake's camp. Raunse, an old shipmate of Drake's, had captured two Spanish ships, which he brought with him. He and his men wanted to join Drake's force.

Drake was pleased. He now had over 100 men. He would need them all, for he had a bold plan. Instead of raiding ships, he wanted to make a surprise attack on Nombre de Dios itself! Although the *flota* had already left for Spain, there were still tons of silver and gold in the town's warehouses.

Early in the morning of July 28, 1572, the raiders rowed silently to the sleeping town. They quickly captured six cannons that protected the port and a ship that had tried to raise an alarm. Then the men entered Nombre de Dios in two groups. They would attack the town square from different directions.

The surprised Spanish did not know the size of the English force. The mayor of Nombre de Dios assembled more than 200 soldiers in the town square. When Drake's men came into view, the Spanish fired. Most of their musket balls missed, but one Englishman was killed and Drake was wounded in the leg. Before the Spaniards could fire again, the English were upon them. The frightened Spanish threw down their weapons and ran for their lives.

Drake and his men controlled Nombre de Dios, but they did not have much time. As soon as the Spanish realized that they outnumbered the pirates, they would return in force. In the mayor's house, Drake's men found a pile of silver bars, each weighing 40 pounds. However, the commander ordered his men to leave them alone. He hoped to find even more in the buildings where treasure was stored.

The heavy warehouse doors were bolted, so Drake ordered his men to break them down. As he stepped forward, his men noticed the blood running down his leg. When the Englishmen saw this, they

Even though Drake urged the men to take the treasure–the warehouses held 360 tons of silver and an even greater amount of gold– his crew felt that their captain's life was worth more than the riches of Nombre de Dios.

became nervous. Despite Drake's protests, they bandaged his leg and returned to the ships.

Although disappointed with the raid's failure, Drake made a quick recovery. He was soon raiding Spanish shipping throughout the Caribbean.

Drake also made an alliance with a group of black men known as the *cimarrones*. These men had been brought from Africa to the Caribbean as slaves but had escaped from their Spanish masters. They lived in hiding throughout the Central American jungles. The *cimarrones* gave Drake valuable information about Spanish treasure trains.

In January 1573, Drake learned that the *flota* had landed at Nombre de Dios. This meant mule trains carrying treasure would soon arrive in the city. Drake knew the Spaniards expected him to attack from the sea. He decided to **ambush** one of the treasure trains instead. However, his first attempt at a surprise land attack was unsuccessful.

For the next month, Drake attacked Spanish ships. He wanted his enemies to believe that he had given up his plan to attack by land. Around this time, he met Guillaume Le Testu, a French pirate and explorer. Le Testu had explored the coast of Brazil and published a book of maps, *Cosmographie Universelle*, in 1556. He also was one of

Francis Drake and the English had bad luck in the fall of 1572. First, his brother John was killed trying to capture a Spanish warship. Then, his men started dying from an unknown disease. Nearly 30 men died, including Francis's younger brother Joseph.

the first people to export tobacco from the New World to Europe. Drake and Le Testu agreed to work together and attack a Spanish treasure train.

In April 1573, a small force made up of English and French pirates and *cimarrones* set an ambush about a mile east of Nombre de Dios. This time, they caught the Spanish completely by surprise. The pirates captured over 25 tons of silver and gold, worth more than $5 million.

Drake knew the Spanish would give chase, so his men buried the silver. Le Testu, who had been wounded during the raid, stayed behind with two

This map of Florida and the Caribbean was made by
Guillaume Le Testu. When Drake met Le Testu, the
Frenchman had already been raiding Spanish settlements
in the West Indies for years.

men. The rest headed for the coast, carrying as much gold as they could.

Drake had picked a spot along the coast to meet his ships. However, when they arrived at this point, the English pinnaces were not there.

Drake ordered a raft to be built out of driftwood.

Then, leaving most of the party in a hiding place, he and three others sailed out to sea to find the English ships. It was a dangerous trip on a frail craft through shark-infested waters. Few of the men thought they would ever see their captain again.

Drake followed the coast for about six miles before spotting his pinnaces anchored in a sheltered cove. At first, the men on the English ships thought the raid had failed. But when Drake climbed aboard one of the pinnaces, he broke into a large smile and pulled out some gold. His men cheered! Drake then directed the pinnaces to pick up the stranded men.

The raid was not a complete success. Spanish troops searching for Drake and his men had killed Le Testu and recovered the silver. However, even after the treasure was divided between the English and French pirates, Drake had about $3 million in gold to take home.

Before sailing home, Drake could not resist one last insult. He sailed his ship back and forth across the harbor at Cartagena as the Spaniards within quaked with fear. Then he headed east to England.

On Sunday, August 9, 1573, church services in Plymouth were interrupted by exciting news from the harbor. Francis Drake had come home.

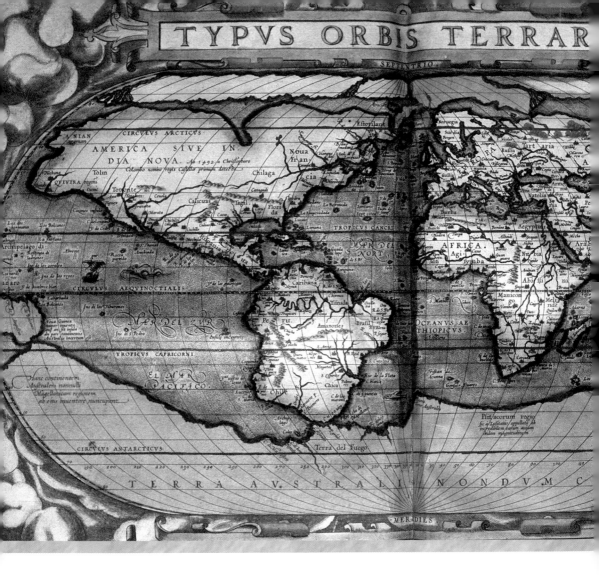

Around the
World

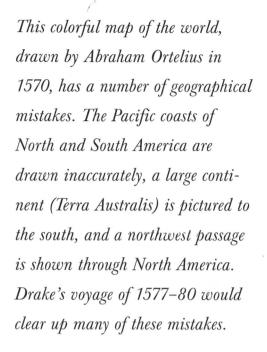

This colorful map of the world, drawn by Abraham Ortelius in 1570, has a number of geographical mistakes. The Pacific coasts of North and South America are drawn inaccurately, a large continent (Terra Australis) is pictured to the south, and a northwest passage is shown through North America. Drake's voyage of 1577–80 would clear up many of these mistakes.

4

When Drake returned to England, his mind was on the Pacific Ocean. Because ships rarely ventured into the Pacific, Spain's outposts on the coast would not be as well defended as the towns in the Caribbean, Drake reasoned. A surprise attack could yield a lot of treasure.

Few men had ever sailed through the vast Pacific Ocean. The first European to sail from the Atlantic to the Pacific had been a Portuguese captain named Ferdinand

Magellan. In 1519, Magellan had led an expedition of five Spanish ships west in search of a passage through the Americas to the East Indies. After months of searching, Magellan found a **strait**, or sea passage, between the Atlantic and Pacific Oceans. It was located near the southern tip of South America.

After sailing cautiously through the treacherous strait, Magellan and his men sailed across the vast Pacific Ocean. Finally, they reached a group of islands he named the Philippines. Magellan was killed during a battle with natives in the islands, but one of his ships did manage to return to Spain. The men sailed west through the Indian Ocean, around Africa, and north through the Atlantic. This made Magellan's expedition the first to sail completely around, or **circumnavigate**, the world.

Magellan's route to the East Indies was long and dangerous. It was safer and more profitable for Spain to exploit the riches of the New World than to sail to China and India on the long Pacific route. As a result, the Strait of Magellan was hardly used.

By 1576, the time seemed right for Drake to sail to the Pacific. However, he would need Queen Elizabeth's support. Drake befriended several of the queen's advisors. They told Elizabeth about Drake's

*The 1519–22 expedition of
Ferdinand Magellan was
the first to encircle the globe.
Magellan did not survive
[...] however. He*

she agreed to
ld include an

..

had to be kept
Drake official
d towns. This
lizabeth did not
ouble, the queen
not known what

ueen's support a
tell his own men
ilors thought they
Mediterranean Sea.

In the summer of 1576, Drake began preparing for the voyage. In Plymouth, he directed the construction of a new ship, the *Pelican*. It probably was about 70 feet long and had a crew of 80 men. The *Pelican* carried 18 cannons and was built with an extra-strong hull. From this flagship, Drake would command his other ships. They included the *Elizabeth* and the *Marigold*, each with 16 guns; the five-gun *Swan*; and the pinnace *Benedict*.

The experienced crew included one man who had been to the Pacific before—as a prisoner of the Spanish. Drake's younger brother Thomas and his

Sir Christopher Hatton was one of Queen Elizabeth's most influential advisors. He was a friend of Francis Drake and supported plans for his 1577 voyage. Drake was so grateful that he eventually renamed his largest ship Golden Hind, *because Hatton's family crest pictured a gold deer.*

15-year-old cousin John were aboard the *Pelican*. Also, a number of gentlemen had joined the voyage. Most were just out for adventure, although one, Drake's friend Thomas Doughty, knew where the ships were really going.

On December 13, 1577, Francis Drake led his ships

Francis Drake planned to sail west through the Strait of Magellan, then head north along the coast of South America to Peru. He would seize Spanish treasure, then return to England the way he had come.

out of Plymouth harbor. The *Pelican* led the way south. The sailors soon realized plans had been changed when they did not enter the Mediterranean. Instead, they sailed for the coast of Africa.

The first stop was the Cape Verde Islands, off the coast of Africa. There Drake captured a Portuguese ship, the *Santa Maria*. Drake filled the ship with his own men and renamed the vessel *Mary*, after his wife. He kept the ship's Portuguese pilot, Nuño da Silva, aboard. Silva was an experienced sailor who was familiar with the Pacific. The rest of the Portuguese crew was set afloat in a pinnace.

Drake made Thomas Doughty captain of the *Mary*. A short time later, he promoted Doughty again, this time to command of the flagship *Pelican*. However, their friendship started to become strained. Doughty wanted to take over command of the voyage. He tried to stir some of the sailors to **mutiny** against Drake. When the captain learned about Doughty's plan, he sent him to the *Swan*.

Even though he had been relieved of command, Doughty was not imprisoned. He was free to roam the *Swan* as he wished, and he continued to speak about mutiny against Drake. Here he had an audience, because the *Swan*'s crew included a number of gentlemen. These men refused to do any work on the ship, which angered the common sailors during the long voyage across the Atlantic.

After 60 days at sea, the ships sighted the coast of South America. Drake's ships stopped several times as they sailed south along the coast toward the Strait of Magellan. In June, they visited Port San Julián. This was a sheltered harbor where Ferdinand Magellan had spent the winter of 1519–20.

Drake knew that the next part of the voyage would be the most difficult. He had two problems to deal with: Thomas Doughty, and the gentlemen who refused to work. On June 30, 1578, Drake accused Doughty of attempting to incite a mutiny.

He appointed a jury to decide Doughty's fate. After hearing testimony, the jury found Doughty guilty and sentenced him to die on July 2, 1578.

Before the execution, Drake and Doughty ate together in a private cabin. Perhaps they resolved their differences, for as Doughty knelt before the executioner's block, he prayed aloud that the voyage would succeed. Then the axe fell, lopping off his head.

Like Drake, Ferdinand Magellan had faced a possible mutiny. Magellan executed the ringleaders at Port San Julián. When Drake's ships sailed into the narrow harbor, the wooden frame Magellan had used to hang the mutineers 58 years earlier was still standing.

Some six weeks later, Drake was ready to leave Port San Julián. Because he no longer had enough men to sail all of his ships, Drake decided to destroy the *Swan* and *Mary*. He divided the sailors and supplies among the *Pelican*, *Elizabeth*, and *Marigold*. Drake then spoke to the entire crew. He told them he expected both common sailors and gentlemen to share in the work. He also reminded them that their voyage was being made for the glory of the queen and England.

"Lo, this is the end of traitors," Drake told his men, displaying the head of Thomas Doughty. The death of Doughty ended all talk of mutiny on the voyage.

On August 24, 1578, Drake's fleet arrived at the entrance to the Strait of Magellan. Drake held a brief ceremony, during which he changed the name of the ship *Pelican* to *Golden Hind.* The English ships then sailed forward into the dangerous strait.

The 334-mile passage between the Atlantic and Pacific Oceans was one of the most dangerous in the world. It was narrow, rocky, and twisting. In some areas, the water was so shallow that boats were in danger of running aground. Other places were too deep to anchor. Despite the dangers, Drake and his men picked their way through the strait in 14 days. This was more than three weeks faster than it had taken Magellan. The three ships then turned to the north, seeking the coast of Chile.

A powerful storm hit shortly after Drake's ships entered the Pacific Ocean. For nearly two months, the ships were blown south. One stormy night, the *Marigold* sank with all hands. Then the *Elizabeth* and *Golden Hind* were separated. *Elizabeth*'s captain decided to sail back through the strait and return to England. Drake's ship was now alone in the Pacific.

It was at this time that Drake would make an important geographical discovery. Sailing south to avoid the storms, he discovered the southernmost tip of South America. Geographers had believed that to the south of the Strait of Magellan was a large continent called Terra Australis. Drake proved that if there was a Terra Australis, it lay farther south. He also claimed a group of uninhabited islands for his country, naming them the Elizabeth Islands.

When the storm finally ended on October 28,

1578, Drake swung his ship to the north again. Many of the sailors were suffering from a disease called *scurvy*, caused by the lack of fresh fruit in their diets. The disease made the sailors' arms and legs ache, and their gums became painfully swollen. Several men died from scurvy.

Nevertheless, Drake set a course north. He stopped once along the coast of Chile. At first the natives were friendly, but then they attacked. Four English sailors were killed and six others were wounded. Drake himself was hit with an arrow under his right eye.

The English had better luck when they reached the Spanish settlements farther to the north. The *Golden Hind* attacked the Spanish ports of Valparaiso, Arica, Chule, and Callao, capturing some treasure. At Callao, Drake learned that the *Nuestra Señora de la Concepción*, a ship loaded with silver, had just left a few days before. He decided to try and catch the Spanish treasure ship.

The *Nuestra Señora de la Concepción* had a three-day head start. Drake promised a gold chain to the crewman who spotted the ship first. On March 1, 1579, Drake's young cousin John, a lookout, spotted a sail several miles ahead. The English pulled alongside and boarded the unarmed ship, capturing it without a fight. On board, Drake discovered an incredible treasure worth more than $7 million. It took several days for this rich cargo of silver to be transferred to the *Golden Hind.*

Drake followed up this great success by capturing several other ships along the western coast of Mexico. But now he was beginning to think about how he would get home. The Spanish were surely sending warships to capture him, so returning through the Strait of Magellan seemed too dangerous. The alternative was to continue sailing to the west, across the Pacific and around the world.

Drake continued to sail north along the coast of Central and North America. During this part of the journey he made his second important geographical discovery. Many people believed there was a northwest passage through the continent. Drake sailed farther to the north than had any other European, but he did not find a northwest passage.

On June 17, 1579, Drake landed in a large bay on the coast of California, probably near the present-day city of San Francisco. Drake claimed the land for England and named it New Albion. During the next five weeks, sailors pulled the *Golden Hind* onto

A replica of Drake's ship, the Golden Hind, *sails alone into the Pacific at sunset.*

the shore and repaired its hull. Drake also sent out small groups to explore the unknown land.

Once the ship was repaired and loaded with food and fresh water, Drake was ready to depart. The next part of the journey–the Pacific crossing–was the most dangerous. Fortunately, Drake had taken some maps from a captured Spanish ship. These showed him the best route across the vast ocean.

For 68 days, the English sailors were out of sight of land. Finally, on September 30, 1579, they spotted a small island. Soon they passed through the chain of some 1,600 islands known as the Philippines. Drake did not stop; he made for the Spice Islands (also called the Moluccas). Valuable items such as pepper, nutmeg, mace, cinnamon, and cloves were shipped from these islands to Europe, where they were sold for an enormous profit.

Although Portugal controlled the spice trade, Drake asked to meet with the ruler of the Moluccas, the Sultan of Ternate. The two men made a deal: England would help free the Spice Islands from Portuguese control, and in return the English would receive exclusive trade rights.

The rest of the voyage home was filled with danger. At one point the ship crashed into an underwater *coral reef* and was damaged, but the sailors pumped out the water and repaired the hole in the ship. After sailing across the Indian Ocean, the Englishmen spotted the coast of Africa. They sailed around the Cape of Good Hope and headed north to England. The final leg of the historic journey had taken nearly a year. It was September 26, 1580, when the battered *Golden Hind* sailed into Plymouth harbor, loaded with treasure. Francis Drake's reputation as England's greatest naval hero was assured.

Humbling the Armada

This colorful painting shows a confused battle between the English navy and the powerful Spanish armada. Sir Francis Drake is often credited with saving England from the armada, even though he was only second in command of the English fleet.

5

In the five years after his voyage around the world, Francis Drake remained close to home. His fame continued to grow. He was elected to **Parliament**, an assembly of English noblemen and commoners that made the country's laws. The queen also named him to a special board overseeing the operations of England's navy. In 1584, he was asked to capture some Dutch pirates who were attacking English ships in the English Channel.

Things were not all good, though. In 1582 Drake's cousin John was captured by the Spanish. The next year, Drake's beloved wife Mary died.

In 1585, Drake married for the second time. His beautiful young wife, Elizabeth Sydenham, was a member of one of the richest families in England.

He did not stay home with his new wife for long, however. In September 1585 Drake raided the Cape Verde Islands and the West Indies. His men captured Santo Domingo, the most important Spanish outpost in the New World. They also hit Cartagena, which Drake took in a surprise attack.

Drake sailed along the coast of North America before turning for home. He stopped to destroy the Spanish fort at St. Augustine, Florida. Drake then visited the English colony at Roanoke Island, off the coast of North Carolina, and brought the colonists back to England. Drake returned home in July 1586.

Drake's bold voyage angered the king of Spain. The English sailor had stolen treasure that could

Sir Walter Raleigh had established the Roanoke Island colony, England's first in the New World. When Drake visited, the colonists were running out of supplies and wanted to go home.

have been used to fortify Philip's empire. Drake's voyage had also inspired other English captains to attack Spanish ships. King Philip decided it was time to end the English naval threat. He began preparing an **armada**, a large fleet of ships. The armada would smash the English navy, then Philip's army would invade the island.

Drake warned the queen about the Spanish invasion force. He asked for money, ships, and men to strike at Spain before the armada could sail. However, Queen Elizabeth still hoped that a diplomatic solution could be found. Finally, in 1587 she allowed Drake to make another voyage. He would command 24 ships and 3,000 men—the largest fleet he had ever led. His mission was to disrupt Spain's preparations for the invasion of England.

Drake sailed first to the Spanish port of Cadiz. There, he sank or captured numerous ships, stole cannons and other weapons, and destroyed food and supplies intended for the armada. Next, he stopped at Sagres, on the coast of Portugal, where he destroyed 47 ships. In a final insult, Drake's ships blockaded Lisbon, where the armada was assembling. For several days, no Spanish ships could get into or out of the harbor. And on the way back to

England, he captured a Spanish ship, the *San Felipe*, that was filled with gold, silver, spices, and other treasures from the East Indies.

Drake's voyage kept the armada from sailing for a year. However, Philip was still determined to crush England. In May 1588, the armada set sail for the English Channel. It was the largest European fleet ever assembled up to that time, with 93 large warships and about 40 smaller warships. The ships were generally larger than the English ships. Many of them were galleys, ships that could be rowed into position with long oars. The ships of the armada carried 19,000 soldiers. In battle, the Spanish planned to pull alongside English ships, board them with the soldiers, and capture the vessels.

To meet them, the English had assembled a fleet of 51 larger ships and numerous smaller ships. The overall commander was Lord Howard of Effingham, and Drake was named second in command. The English fleet was divided into four squadrons, with Howard, Drake, John Hawkins, and Martin Frobisher each commanding a group.

Although the English fleet was smaller, its ships were faster, more maneuverable, and better armed. They could sail away from Spanish ships trying to

This drawing from an English book about the Spanish armada shows the armada in its crescent formation being pursued through the English Channel by four groups of ships. Drake led one of the English squadrons; the others were commanded by Lord Howard, John Hawkins, and Martin Frobisher.

board and fire on the armada from a distance.

The Spanish ships sailed slowly into the English Channel. They formed a huge, imposing crescent, with the strongest warships in the center. The lead ship was the enormous *San Martin,* which carried the armada's commander, the Duke of Medina Sidonia. The line of ships was nearly two miles wide. As night fell on July 20, Drake and Howard led 54 ships along the coast in the darkness. They managed to get behind the armada without being noticed. On the morning of July 21, they had the wind at their backs and were ready to attack.

During the first day of fighting, neither side could take control of the battle. The ships of the armada were not able to get close enough to the speedy English ships to board and capture them. However, the English ships stayed too far out of range for their cannons to inflict much damage. After four hours, the fighting ended. No ships had been sunk on either side, but the English were able to drive the Spanish ships past Plymouth.

As the armada sailed through the English Channel, one large ship, the *San Salvador*, caught fire. Gunpowder on board exploded, destroying the ship. Then the *Nuestra Señora del Rosario*, one of the largest ships in the armada, was damaged in a collision with another vessel. Its mast cracked, and the *Nuestra Señora del Rosario* dropped behind the other ships. Its captain steered toward the coast to try and avoid the pursuing English ships.

As night fell, Drake noticed the lights of the *Nuestra Señora del Rosario*. He was afraid the Spanish were trying the same trick the English had pulled the night before—sailing behind the fleet in order to attack with the wind in the morning. In his ship *Revenge*, he sailed cautiously over to investigate. He found the damaged *Nuestra Señora del Rosario*. Even though the ship was twice as large as Drake's *Revenge*, the Spanish captain surrendered.

For the next four days, the English continued to harass the Spanish fleet. They did not cause much damage, but they were able to drive the armada past the Isle of Wight. The Duke of Medina Sidonia had wanted to capture this island to use it as a base for the Spanish army's attack on England. He was frustrated by the English tactics. "The enemy has resolutely avoided coming to close quarters with our ships, although I have tried my hardest to make him do so," he wrote to a Spanish general. He ordered his fleet to anchor in the French port of Calais.

Around midnight on July 28, eight English ships were pulled into a line aimed at the anchored Spanish ships. After the sails were raised and the rudders tied into position, the crews lit fuses and climbed out of the ships into waiting boats. As the eight large ships sailed toward the armada, flames began to appear on the decks. The burning ships were soon

The *Nuestra Señora del Rosario* was quite a prize. It had 52 cannons and carried 450 sailors. On board, Drake found more than 20,000 ducats—one-third of the money carried by the armada.

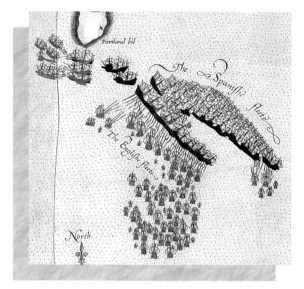

The Battle of Gravelines, on July 29, 1588, was the decisive encounter with the Spanish armada. The English sank at least five ships, killing 1,500 Spaniards and capturing 800 others.

among the ships of the armada. The panicked Spaniards cut their anchors and tried to avoid being rammed. By dawn, the armada was totally disorganized. Then the English fleet, now up to 140 ships, attacked. The Battle of Gravelines, as the fighting on July 29 became known, would be the turning point. The English sank a number of ships, killed 1,500 Spaniards, and captured 800 soldiers and sailors.

Frustrated, the Duke of Medina Sidonia sailed for home. On the way, the Spanish ships were separated in a storm off the coast of Ireland. By the time the armada limped back to Spain, 60 of its 130 ships had been lost and 15,000 men killed. For King Philip, the destruction of his armada was devastating: "If God does not send a miracle . . . I hope to die and go to him . . . which is what I pray for, so as not to see so much ill fortune and disgrace."

With the English victory over the Spanish armada, Sir Francis Drake was the most famous man in England. But he was not ready to relax. Drake wanted to follow up the victory over the armada with an English invasion of Portugal. However, this attack in the spring of 1589 was no more successful than the Spanish invasion attempt had been. Disappointed, Drake returned home.

With England safe from invasion, Elizabeth had no interest in ambitious naval attacks, so Drake decided to retire to Plymouth. He was elected again to Parliament, where he spent the next five years.

As Plymouth's representative, Drake arranged for fortifications to be built that would protect the town from attack, and he oversaw the construction of a 17-mile channel that would bring fresh water to the town from a river inland. He also continued to plan another foray against Spain.

> According to legend, when the Plymouth channel was completed, Drake rode through it on horseback just ahead of a wave of water as crowds cheered. The channel carried water to the town for 300 years.

This statue of Sir Francis Drake, England's greatest naval hero, looks out to sea from Plymouth. Legend has it that when England is in danger, Drake's spirit will return to help the Britons defend their island.

In 1595, Elizabeth finally gave permission for an English raid on Spanish possessions in the New World. She named Drake and Sir John Hawkins co-commanders. This seemed like a chance for the two great English seamen to gain revenge for their defeat at San Juan de Ulúa 27 years earlier.

The expedition was troubled from the start. Drake and Hawkins did not agree on how the attack should be carried out. During the voyage, the two leaders argued constantly about tactics. But by the time the fleet was ready to attack San Juan, an important Spanish town on the island of Puerto

Rico, Drake was in sole command. Hawkins had become sick and died on the voyage. Many of the English sailors had become sick as well, and the Spanish easily repulsed their attack.

The Englishmen did destroy several Spanish ports. By this time, though, Drake was among the English sailors suffering from disease. Although he continued to order attacks, he spent most of the time sick in his cabin. Early in the morning of January 28, 1596, Sir Francis Drake died.

As a memorial, the English destroyed the Spanish city of Portobelo, then formally buried their captain at sea. Hundreds of cannons fired a farewell salvo as the waters of the Caribbean closed over the famous adventurer.

The geographical discoveries that Drake made on his voyage around the world were very important. As Spain's power faded, the world's oceans were opened to explorers from England and other European countries. The naval tradition that Drake established in England would enable the small island nation to become a major world power, establishing a colonial empire that spanned the globe.

Chronology

1541   Francis Drake is born in Tavistock, England.

1549   A religious uprising causes Drake's family to flee to Chatham, a suburb of London.

1558   Elizabeth I becomes queen of England.

1564   Drake sets out on first voyage to the West Indies.

1567   Sails to the West Indies with John Hawkins; the voyage turns into a disaster at San Juan de Ulúa the next year.

1569   Drake returns to the Spanish Main as a privateer; marries Mary Newman in Plymouth.

1572   Attempts to capture Spanish treasure train at Nombre de Dios; brothers John and Joseph die in the Caribbean.

1573   Forms partnership with French pirate Le Testu; successfully intercepts treasure train and returns to England.

1577   Sets out with five ships on a voyage to the Pacific Ocean.

1578   Puts down the mutiny of Thomas Doughty; discovers Cape Horn.

1579   Captures Spanish treasure ship *Nuestra Señora de la Concepción*; claims Nova Albion for England.

1580   Returns to England after sailing around the world.

1581   Knighted on the deck of the *Golden Hind*.

1583   Wife Mary Drake dies.

1585   Marries Elizabeth Sydenham; conducts successful raid on Spanish settlements in the West Indies.

1588   Leads English defense against the Spanish armada.

1591   Builds Plymouth watercourse.

1596   Dies at sea during unsuccessful raid on the Spanish Main.

alliance–an agreement between two people or countries to work together for a common cause.

ambush–a surprise attack, usually from a concealed position.

armada–a fleet of warships.

apprentice–a person who is bound to another in order to learn a trade or art.

circumnavigate–to sail around the world.

conquistadors–Spanish soldiers who explored the New World.

coral reefs–large, hard underwater ridges made up of the stony skeletons of sea creatures called coral.

flagship–a ship that carries the commander of a fleet.

mutiny–a revolt by a ship's crew against discipline or against a commanding officer.

navigation–the science of directing the course of a seagoing vessel and of determining its position.

Parliament–an assembly of noblemen and elected representatives that helps England's monarch rule the country.

pinnace–a small sailboat that can be carried in a larger ship, then assembled quickly when needed.

scurvy–a disease caused by lack of vitamin C, which was common on long sea voyages. Its signs include loose teeth, bleeding, and soreness in the arm and leg joints.

spices–any of various aromatic vegetable products, such as pepper or nutmeg, used to season or flavor foods.

strait–a relatively narrow passageway that connects two large bodies of water.

Further Reading

Drake, Sir Francis. *The World Encompassed by Sir Francis Drake.* New York: Harper and Row, 1977.

Duncan, Alice Smith. *Sir Francis Drake and the Struggle for an Ocean Empire.* New York: Chelsea House, 1993.

Gallagher, Jim. *Ferdinand Magellan and the First Voyage Around the World.* Philadelphia: Chelsea House, 2000.

Konstam, August. *Historical Atlas of Exploration, 1492-1600.* New York: Checkmark Books, 2000.

Lewis, Richard S. *From Vinland to Mars: A Thousand Years of Exploration.* New York: Quadrangle Books, 1976.

Sugden, John. *Sir Francis Drake.* New York: Henry Holt, 1991.

Picture Credits

JIM GALLAGHER is the author of more than a dozen books for young adults, including biographies of Vasco da Gama, Ferdinand Magellan, Hernando de Soto, and the Viking explorers in the Chelsea House series EXPLORERS OF NEW WORLDS. A former newspaper editor and publisher, he lives in Stockton, New Jersey.